How to Use This Book

D1540586

Lots of books have maps in them. Many textbooks have [maps] atlas consists almost entirely of maps. This book has map[s] in textbooks and atlases, but it has another kind of map tha[t they don't] have. This book has "practice maps."

Maps with labels help you to learn the names of the contintents, countries, and oceans. Practice maps don't have labels. They help you to practice and quiz yourself so you will remember what you have learned. Practice maps can be used to play geography games with your friends and family.

Here are some ways you can use this book to learn and remember world geography:

> Work on one continent at a time.
> Learn a few countries at a time.
> Make practice an active process.
> Answer the questions provided.
> Make up some questions of your own.
> Point to the countries on the labeled map.
> Point to the countries on the practice map.
> Involve all of your senses:
>
> > • Say their names out loud as you point.
> >
> > • Spell their names out loud.
> >
> > • Write their names on scratch paper.

Use the cut-out pointers at the back of the book to practice. Lay the pointers on the practice maps to show where they are located. Say the names of the countries as you place them on the maps. Say phrases and sentences out loud as you place the pointers, such as:

> "Costa Rica is sixth of the seven Central American countries."
>
> "Portugal is here at the southwest corner of Spain."
>
> "Benin is between Togo and Nigeria."

As you learn more countries, get some friends or family members in on the act. Make a game out of it. Look at page 22 for game ideas involving the pointers.

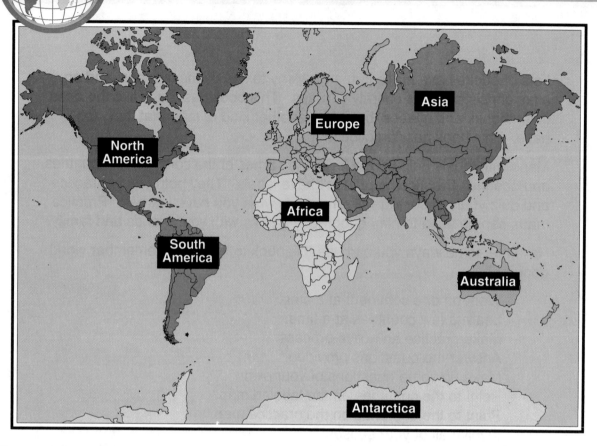

The seven continents are shown below in order of area, starting with the biggest.
Write the name of each continent under its picture

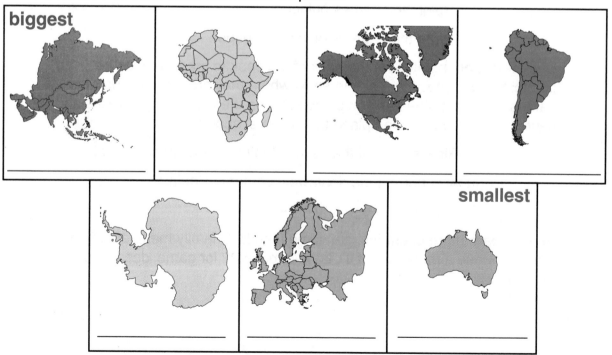

biggest

smallest

_____ _____ _____ _____

_____ _____ _____

Did you notice that a flat map makes areas of land look bigger if they are near the
poles? Compare how Greenland and Antarctica look on a globe.

4152

Comparing Continents: Population

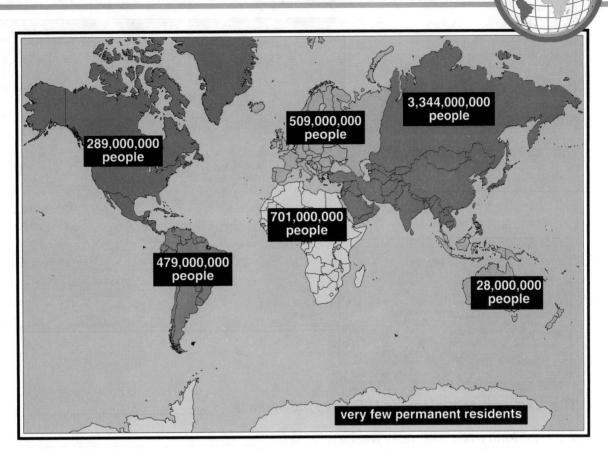

The seven continents are shown below in order of population, starting with the one with the most people. Write the names of each continent.

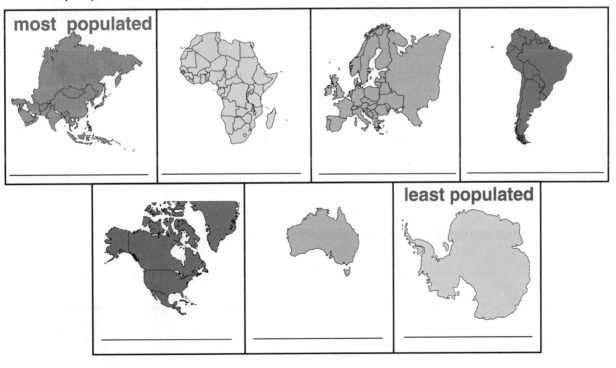

most populated

least populated

Approximately _____ times more people live in Asia than in North America.

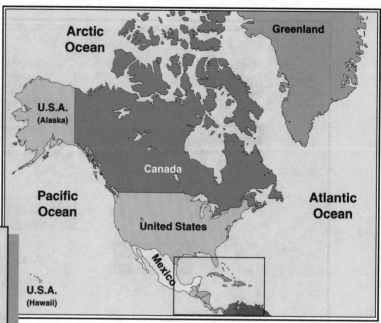

1. The largest country in North America is: _____

2. The northernmost country is:

    _____

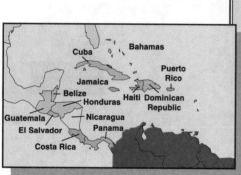

3. The country that borders the U.S.A. to the south is: _____

4. Which country has the most western border? _____

5. Which country is an island in the north Atlantic Ocean? _____

6. Name two parts (states) of the U.S.A. which are separated from the rest of the country: _____   _____

7. Which Central American country connects North America to South America?

    _____

8. Name six countries that are islands near Florida:

    _____   _____

    _____   _____

9. Name the seven small countries between Mexico and South America:

    _____   _____

    _____   _____

    _____   _____

    _____

4152

North America Practice Map

As you come to each practice map, cut out the Pointers (pages 23-31) for that region of the world. Use them to learn the names and locations on the maps.

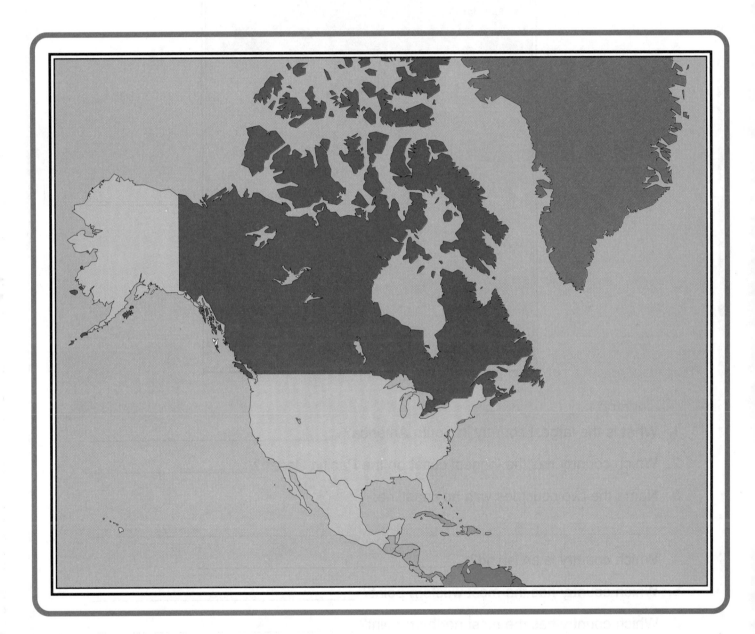

Note: North America Pointers are on page 23.

South American Countries

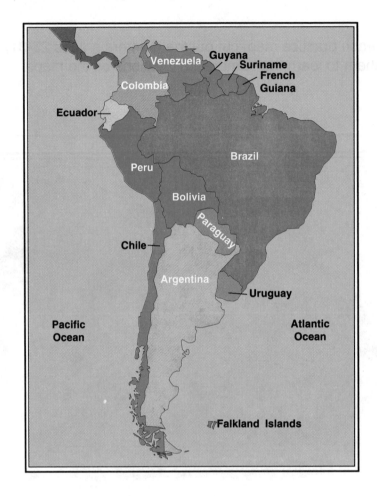

1. What is the largest country in South America? _____

2. Which country has the longest coast on the Pacific Ocean? _____

3. Name the two countries with no coastline:

   _____   _____

4. Which country is an island? _____

5. Which country has the most western point? _____

6. Which country has the most northern point? _____

7. Write the name of the country with a four-letter name: _____

8. List the two countries that do not share a border with Brazil:

   _____

4152

South America Practice Map

Note: South America Pointers are on page 23.

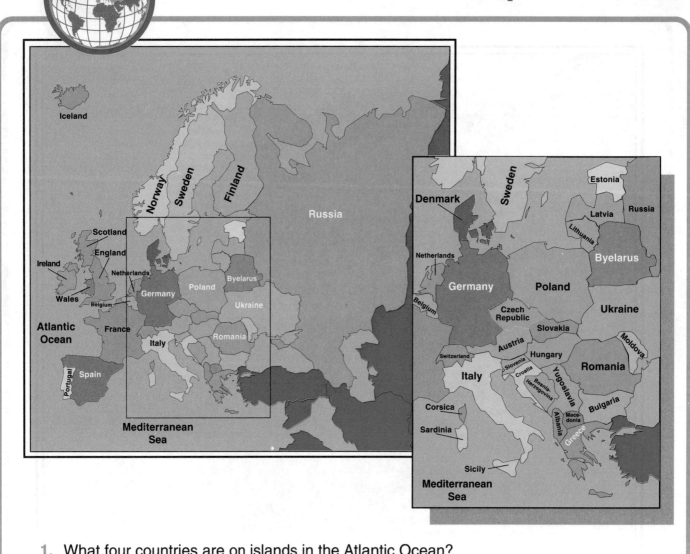

1. What four countries are on islands in the Atlantic Ocean?

   _____   _____

   _____   _____

2. What country looks like a boot in the Mediterranean Sea? _____

3. Name two Italian islands in the Mediterranean Sea:

   _____   _____

4. What three countries are farthest north?   _____

   _____   _____

5. What two countries split the name "Czechoslovakia" to make two new names?

   _____   _____

6. This large country's name begins with the letter "U": _____

Europe Practice Map

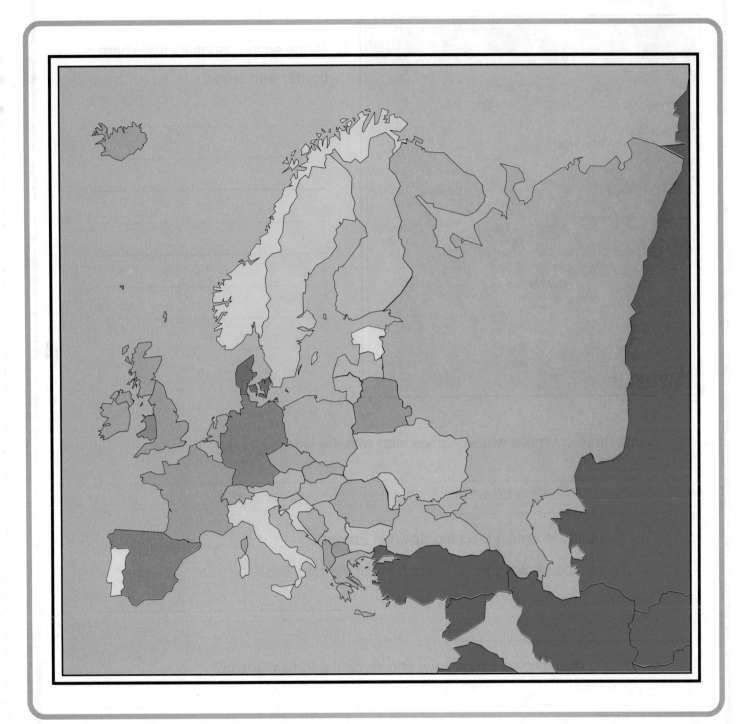

Note: Europe Pointers are on pages 23 and 25.

4152

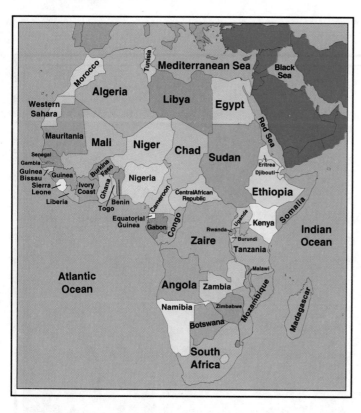

1. Name seven countries that share a border with Niger:

   _____

   _____

   _____

   _____

   _____

   _____

   _____

2. Name three countries whose names start with the letter "Z":

   _____   _____

   _____

3. Which country is almost touching Spain in Europe? _____

4. What countries lie along the western bank of the Red Sea?

   _____   _____

   _____

6. Which five mainland countries have shores on the Indian Ocean?

   _____   _____

   _____   _____

   _____

4152

10

Africa Practice Map

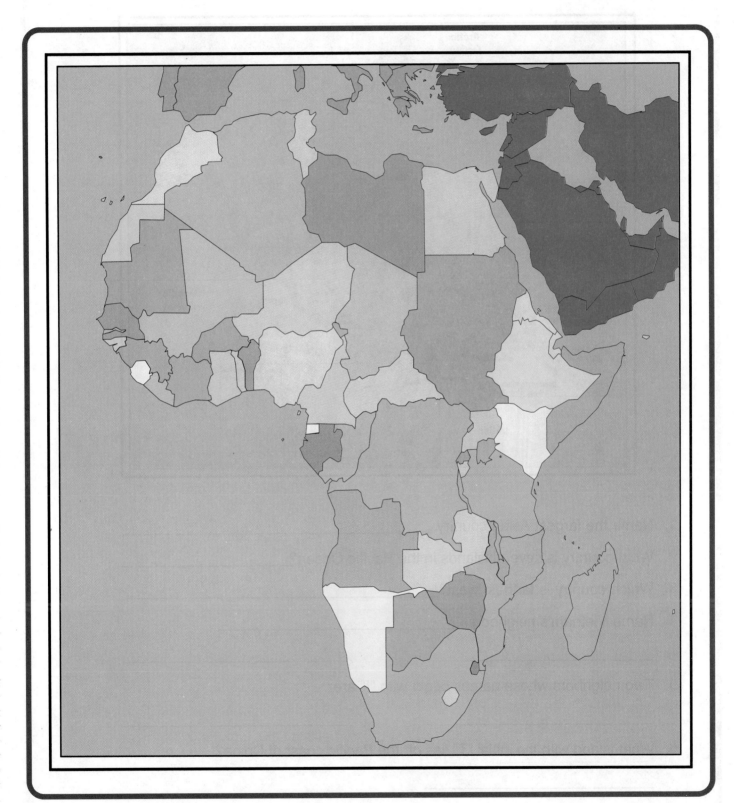

Note: Africa Pointers are on pages 25 and 27.

4152

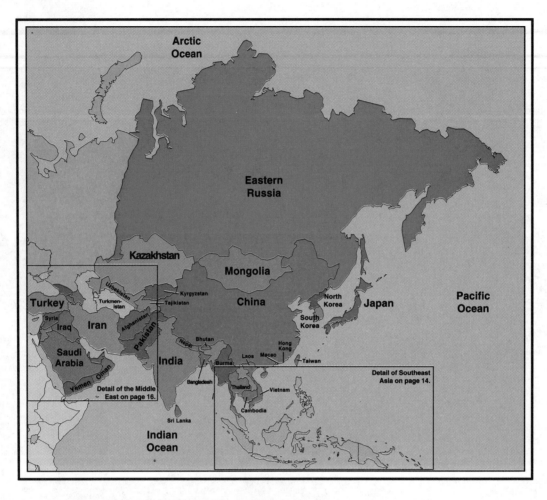

1. Name the largest Asian country: _____

2. What country is several islands in the Pacific Ocean?_____

3. Which country is farthest west?_____

4. Name Vietnam's neighbors: _____

   _____   _____

5. Two neighbors whose names begin with "I" are:

   _____   _____

6. What island with the initial "T" lies off the Pacific coast of China?

   _____

Asia Practice Map

Note: Asia Pointers are on pages 29.

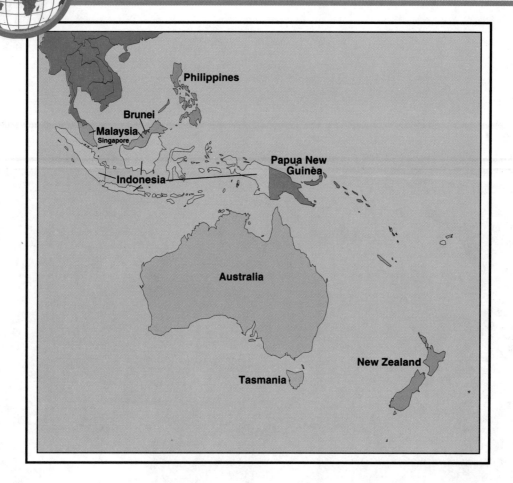

1. Which country is also a continent?_____

2. Which country is divided into several islands and parts of islands?

   _____

3. What is the tiny island nation between the mainland and the island part of

   Malaysia? _____

4. What country south of Australia has a two-word name? _____

5. What country attached to part of Indonesia has a three-word name?

   _____

6. What U.S. ally has a name starting with "Ph"? _____

7. Name the island that is between Australia and New Zealand:_____

8. What is the tiny nation that shares an island with Malaysia and Indonesia?

   _____

4152

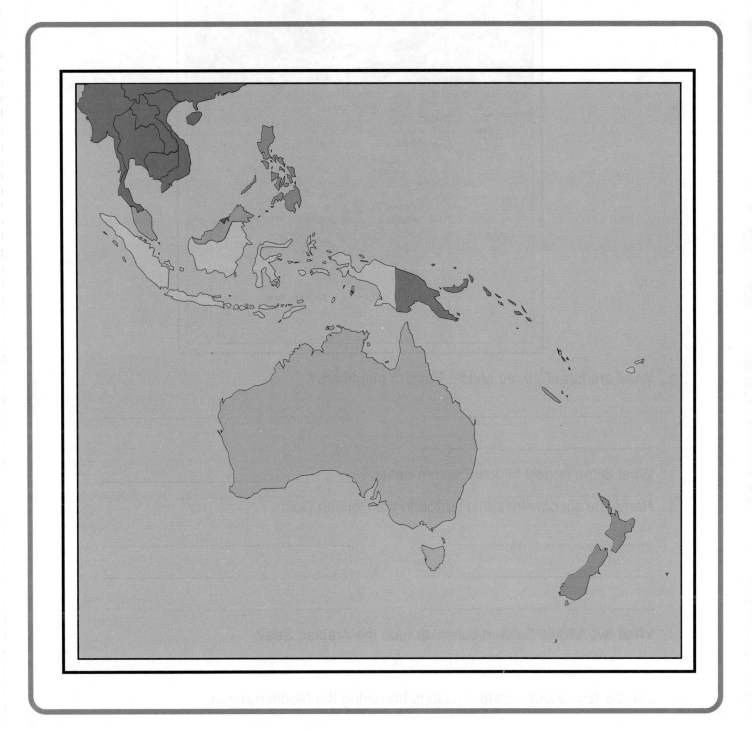

Note: South Pacific Pointers are on page 27.

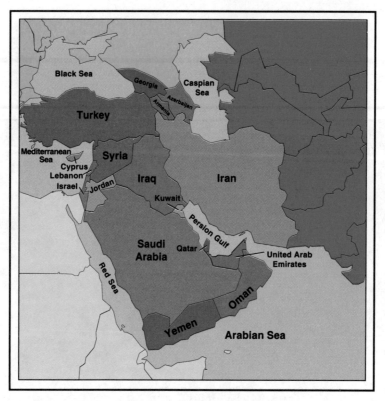

1. What are Israel's three Middle Eastern neighbors?

    _____   _____

    _____

2. What is the largest Middle Eastern nation? _____

3. Name the six countries that surround the Persian Gulf:

    _____   _____

    _____   _____

    _____   _____

4. What two Middle Eastern countries face the Arabian Sea?

    _____   _____

5. List the four Middle Eastern nations bordering the Mediterranean.

    _____   _____

    _____   _____

6. What sea is north of Turkey?_____

7. What sea is north of Iran? _____

Middle East Practice Map

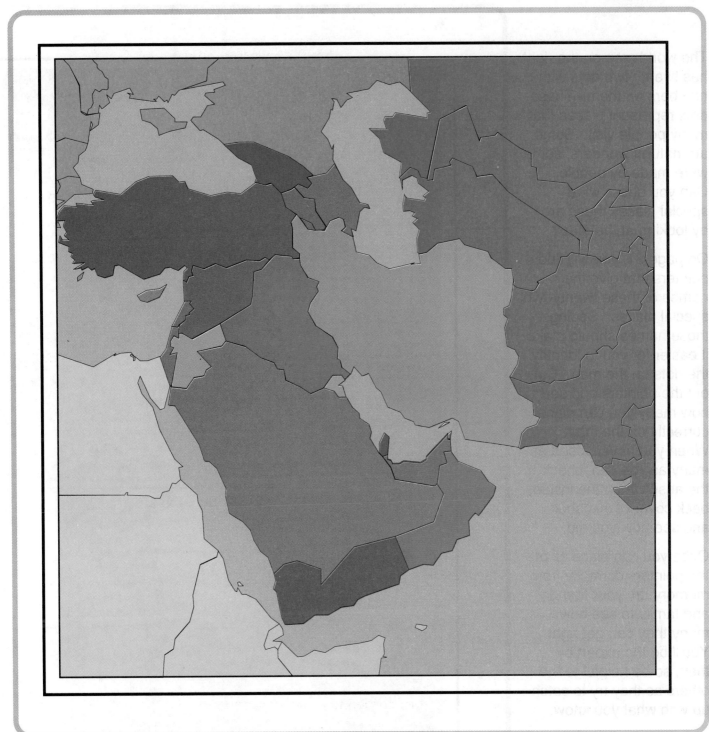

Note: Middle East Pointers are on page 29.

The world map on the right has twenty-two dots with numbers on them. These dots represent places that many people visit. Some are natural wonders; some were made by people. Can you guess what special places these are by looking at the map?

On page 31, you will find pointers that give the names of these twenty-two special places. Seeing those names should make it easier for you to identify the dots on the map. Cut out the pointers and see how many you can place correctly on the map. When you have placed as many as you can, check the answers on the inside back cover of this book and see how you did.

Once you can place all of the pointers correctly from memory, try your friends and family to see how many they can get right. You'll be the expert by then, so be helpful to the others as they try to catch up with what you know.

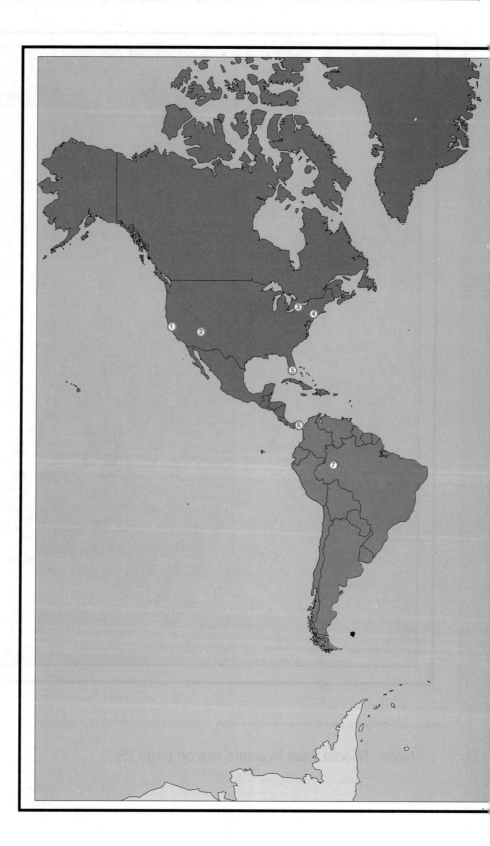

4152

Look At It This Way!

Label the continents and countries that you recognize on this map as viewed from above the North Pole.   What countries can you see that are:

- the farthest south?
- closest to the North Pole?
- closest to the prime meridian?
- closest to the international date line?

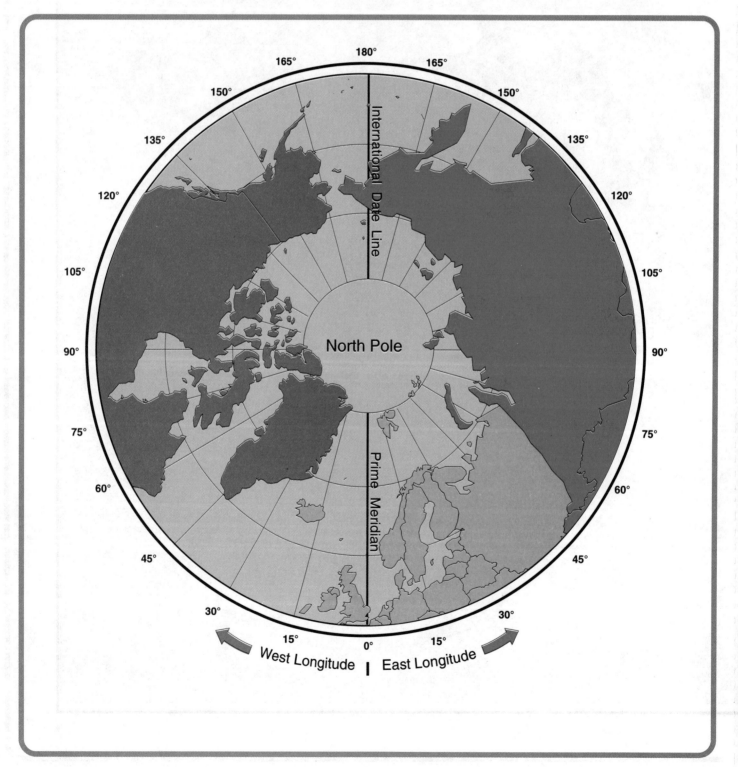

4152

How About This View?

Draw arrows and write labels for them on this map that point the direction to:

- South America
- Africa
- Australia
- Your town

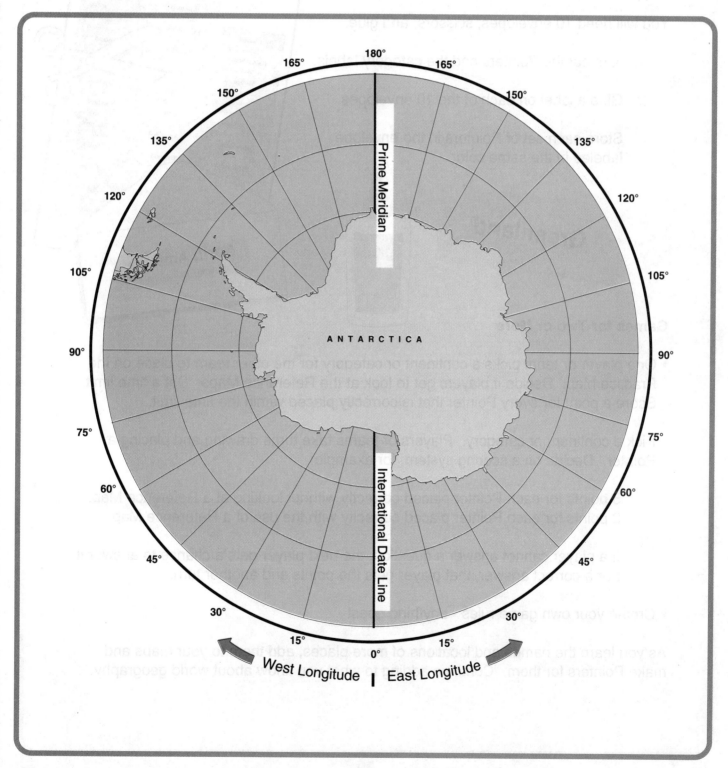

Use the Pointers on pages 23-31 with your Practice Maps to increase your knowledge of World Geography.

Prepare the Pointers for Use

You will need 10 envelopes, scissors, and glue.

1. Cut out the Pointers and the category labels.

2. Glue a label on each of the 10 envelopes.

3. Store each set of Pointers in the envelope labeled in the same color.

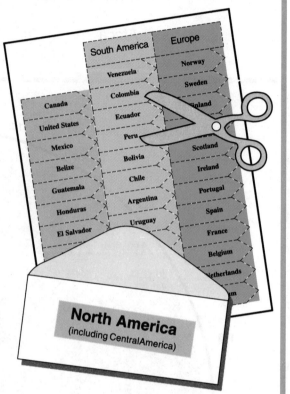

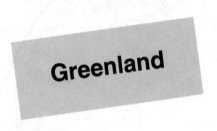

Games for Two or More

- One player or team picks a continent or category for the other team to place on the Practice Map. Decide if players get to look at the Reference Maps. Set a time limit. Score a point for every Pointer that is correctly placed within the time limit.

- Pick a continent or category. Players or teams take turns drawing and placing a Pointer. Decide on a scoring system, for example:

     5 points for each Pointer placed correctly without looking at a Reference Map.
     2 points for each Pointer placed correclty with the use of a Reference Map.

     If a player cannot answer a question, the next player gets a chance to answer it. For a correct answer, that player gets the points and another turn.

- Create your own game rules - anything goes!

As you learn the names and locations of more places, add them to your maps and make Pointers for them. Continue adding to what you know about world geography.

4152

North America (Including Central America)	South America	Europe
Greenland	Venezuela	Norway
Canada	Colombia	Sweden
United States	Ecuador	Finland
Mexico	Peru	England
Belize	Bolivia	Scotland
Guatemala	Chile	Ireland
Honduras	Argentina	Portugal
El Salvador	Uruguay	Spain
Nicaragua	Paraguay	France
Costa Rica	Brazil	Belgium
Panama	French Guiana	Netherlands
Guyana	Suriname	Belgium

4152

Europe		Africa
Germany	Romania	Algeria
Switzerland	Hungary	Lybia
Austria	Czech Republic	Egypt
Slovenia	Slovakia	Morocco
Croatia	Poland	Western Sahara
Serbia	Lithuania	Mauritania
Montenegro	Latvia	Mali
Italy	Estonia	Niger
Greece	Byelorus	Chad
Albania	Ukraine	Sudan
Macedonia	Moldova	Ethiopia
Bulgaria	Russia	Somalia

Africa		South Pacific
Kenya	Gabon	Australia
Tanzania	Central African Republic	New Zealand
Mozambique	Nigeria	Tasmania
South Africa	Malawi	Philippines
Botswana	Ghana	Malaysia
Zimbabwe	Ivory Coast	Indonesia
Namibia	Guinea	Papua New Guinea
Angola	Senegal	Madagascar
Zaire	Gambia	Camaroon
Rwanda	Sierra Leone	Equatorial Guinea
Burundi	Liberia	Uganda
Congo	Togo	Benin

Asia		Middle East
Mongolia	Bhutan	Turkey
China	Bangladesh	Syria
North Korea	Sri Lanka	Lebanon
South Korea	Thailand	Israel
Taiwan	Laos	Jordan
Hong Kong	Vietnam	Saudi Arabia
Macau	Cambodia	Yemen
Japan	Kazakhstan	Iraq
Afghanistan	Uzbekistan	Kuwait
Pakistan	Georgia	Iran
India	Armenia	Qatar
Nepal	Azerbaijan	Oman

4152

Use the pointers on this page to show special places on the World Map on pages 18 and 19. Can you find them all? What are some other places you would like to visit? Add dots for those places and make your own pointers with their names.

Natural Wonders	Human Wonders	Make Some of Your Own
The Great Barrier Reef	Roman Colosseum	
Grand Canyon	Stonehenge	
Victoria Falls	The Parthenon	
Mt. Everest	The Great Wall	
Sahara Desert	Golden Gate Bridge	
Amazon Rainforest	Lenin Square	
Mt. Fuji	The Great Pyramids	
Niagra Falls	The Statue of Liberty	
The Dead Sea	The Taj Majal	
The Everglades	The Eiffel Tower	
Rock of Gibraltar	Panama Canal	